Animal Survivors

by Jack L. Roberts

Table of Contents

Ice Age Animals: Why Some Survived . . . But Most Did Not 4

Unusual Animals of Australia 12

Animal Survival Today 18

Glossary/Index 24

4

12

18

Ice Age Animals:
Why Some Survived . . . But Most Did Not

Imagine living at a time when the land was frozen and little grew. Imagine living where the temperature was below freezing every day. That's what it was like during the Great Ice Age. The Ice Age started over 2 million years ago and ended 11,500 years ago.

During that time, half of North America was covered by giant sheets of ice. According to the National Geographic Society, those ice sheets were more than 3 kilometers (about 2 miles) thick. Many large animals called megafauna[1] roamed the earth then. Some Ice Age animals such as the cougar and musk ox are still found in the wild today. Most Ice Age animals, however, including the saber-toothed tiger and woolly mammoth, died off.

The Basic Needs of All Animals

To survive, every animal on Earth needs food, water, and shelter. The environment, or habitat where they live, gives animals their basic needs. Sometimes, an environment changes. The temperature might get warmer or colder over time. A food source can disappear. Even the physical characteristics can change. For example, forests are destroyed. Rivers dry up. Due to these changes, some animals move to new places. Others adapt and survive. Some can't adapt and die.

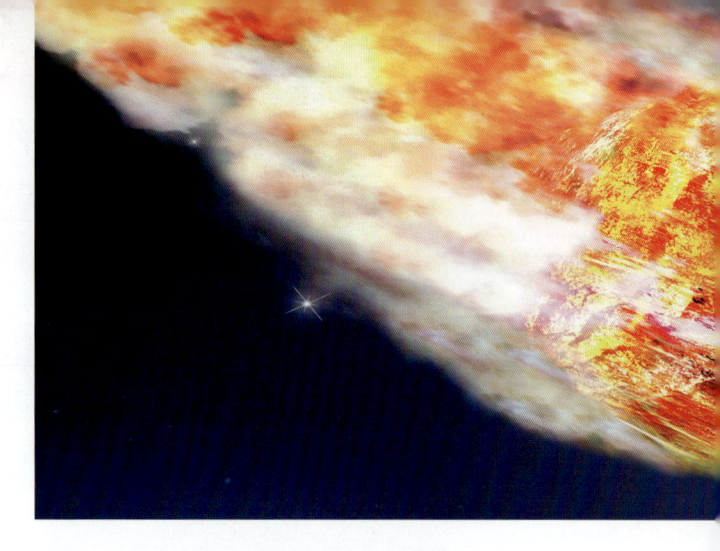

The Disappearance of Ice Age Animals

Scientists are not sure why most of the large animals on Earth died off by the end of the Great Ice Age. Here are some possible causes:

Change in the Weather

Beginning about 50,000 years ago, Earth went through periods of warming up. Then, just as quickly, it would cool down. The megafauna adapted to the cold periods. But during the warming periods, reports *Scientific American* magazine, forests replaced grasslands. With their usual food source gone, some megafauna died off.

1. megafauna—large animals; from the Greek word *mega*, meaning "large," and the Latin word *fauna*, meaning "animal"

Some scientists believe megafauna extinction began 12,000 years ago after a three-mile-wide comet exploded over southern Canada.

Humans

By the end of the Great Ice Age, humans were learning to hunt. Beth Shapiro teaches biology at Penn State University. She says it is likely that people "kept the megafauna from surviving." In addition to killing these large animals, humans hunted the smaller animals that the large animals ate.

A Natural Disaster

Richard Firestone is a scientist at the Berkeley Lab. In 2007 he and other researchers presented a new idea of what wiped out megafauna. They believe a comet[2] exploded over southern Canada. Huge wildfires spread across most of the Northern Hemisphere as a result.

After the fires died out, plants could not grow on the land. The large animals did not have enough to eat.

2. comet—an object in space made of ice and dust. When it passes by the sun, it grows a bright "tail."

Ice Age Losers and Winners

The woolly mammoth, ground sloth, and many other mammals did not survive the Ice Age. They became extinct. The chart below tells about some of these species. It tells why they died off. Then read about four Ice Age animals that are still around.

ICE AGE ANIMAL	ABOUT THE ANIMAL	CAUSES FOR EXTINCTION
American cave lion	one of the most feared large predators; could take down much larger animals	decline of food source; human hunters
giant short-faced bear	largest meat-eating land animal in North America	explosion of a comet caused wildfires and destroyed food sources
woolly rhino	large, heavy animal with thick, shaggy hair and two horns on its nose	climate change; disease; human hunters
woolly mammoth	huge, hairy, elephant-like mammal with tusks up to 4 meters (13 ft.) long	disease; human hunters; natural disaster
giant ground sloth	an ancient sloth as big as today's elephant	human hunters; disappearance of natural habitat
saber-toothed tiger	one of six species of big cats that lived in North America during the Ice Age	lost its primary food source; didn't adapt to new food source

The upper teeth of the saber-toothed tiger were up to 18 centimeters (7 inches) long.

The upper teeth of a jaguar are about 5 cm (2 in).

Cougar and Jaguar

Dr. Larisa R. G. DeSantis studies the big cats of the Great Ice Age. Six species of large cats roamed the plains and forests of North America then. Only the cougar and jaguar survived.

"They were not picky eaters," explains Dr. DeSantis. Their teeth were sharp and strong. So they were able to eat flesh *and* bones of many different prey.

The saber-toothed tiger's teeth, by comparison, "were brittle," adds Dr. DeSantis.

"They would break easily. Therefore, the saber-toothed tiger needed to eat mostly tender meat. They favored mastodons—huge, hairy elephants."

By the end of the Great Ice Age, though, saber-toothed tigers' food source was disappearing. They were not able to adapt. They did not change their diet. So saber-toothed tigers did not survive.

Musk Ox

Despite the word "ox" in its name, the musk ox is not a relative of oxen or cattle. It is a relative of sheep and goats. This Ice Age survivor currently lives in the Arctic. This area around the North Pole is one of the coldest places on Earth.

A coat of long, shaggy hair helps musk oxen survive in the cold. It covers a second layer of hair that provides even more warmth. Yet lots of Ice Age animals had long hair and extra layers of fat. Why did musk oxen survive? The answer, according to Professor Shapiro, may simply be "good luck." Musk oxen lived far from human hunters.

North America   Asia
                       the Arctic

▲ Laws today protect musk oxen. More than 100,000 now live in the wild.

Coyote

The coyote is related to dogs, wolves, and foxes. During the Ice Age, coyotes were much bigger than they are today. Julie Meachen is a researcher at the National Science Foundation. She says that coyotes back then were the size of a wolf. They weighed 36 to 54 kg (80 to 120 lb.).

Today, coyotes weigh 14 to 18 kg (30 to 40 lb.). They grew smaller in the past 10,000 years because "their diet changed," Meachen explains. "During the Ice Age, coyotes ate large animals. But those large animals died off. Coyotes began eating small animals such as rabbits and rodents." Because they adapted to a new food source, coyotes survived.

Conclusion

The Ice Age was a mysterious time. Scientists study this period in history to find clues about animal adaptations and survival in a changing environment.

▲ Coyotes adapted to changes at the end of the Ice Age. Now, they are adapting to living in suburban areas.

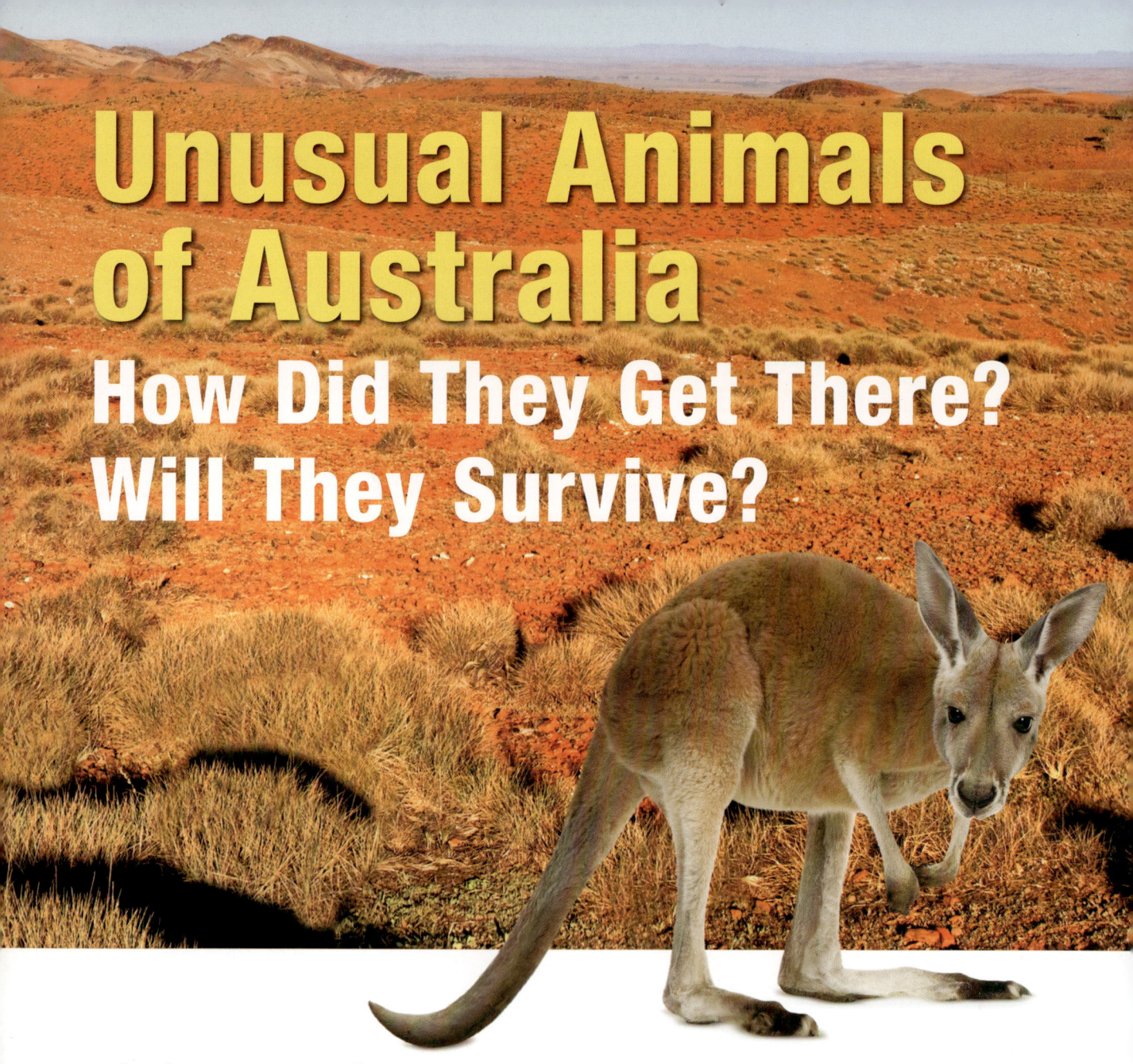

Unusual Animals of Australia
How Did They Get There? Will They Survive?

The kangaroo is the unofficial national animal of Australia. This large, hopping marsupial is found only there and on some other islands nearby. Australia is home to other unusual marsupials. They include the wombat, wallaby, and koala.

Scientists thought that kangaroos and other marsupials developed in Australia millions of years ago. Then, in 1993, scientists discovered a fossil tooth in South America from a platypus, another unusual animal found only in Australia.

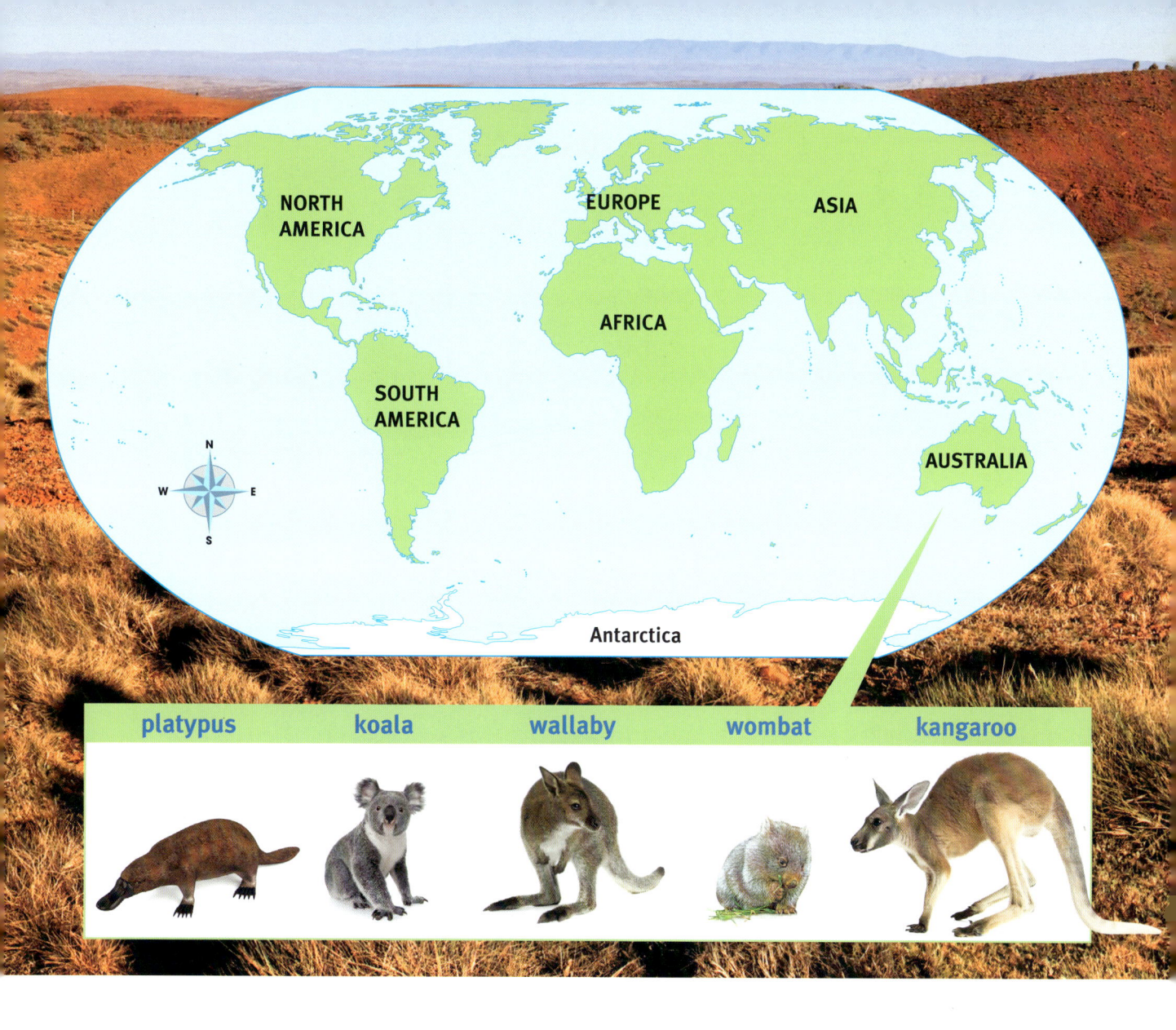

NORTH AMERICA **EUROPE** **ASIA** **AFRICA** **SOUTH AMERICA** **AUSTRALIA** Antarctica

| platypus | koala | wallaby | wombat | kangaroo |

That single tooth changed scientists' thinking. They concluded that ancestors of kangaroos and other Australian animals had lived in South America more than 50 million years ago. Scientists then wondered how those animals got from South America to Australia.

The answer may have to do with how Australia became a continent. "About 300 million years ago, Earth didn't have seven continents," reports LiveScience.com. "Instead, there was one huge supercontinent. In the 1920s, scientists named it Pangaea."

13

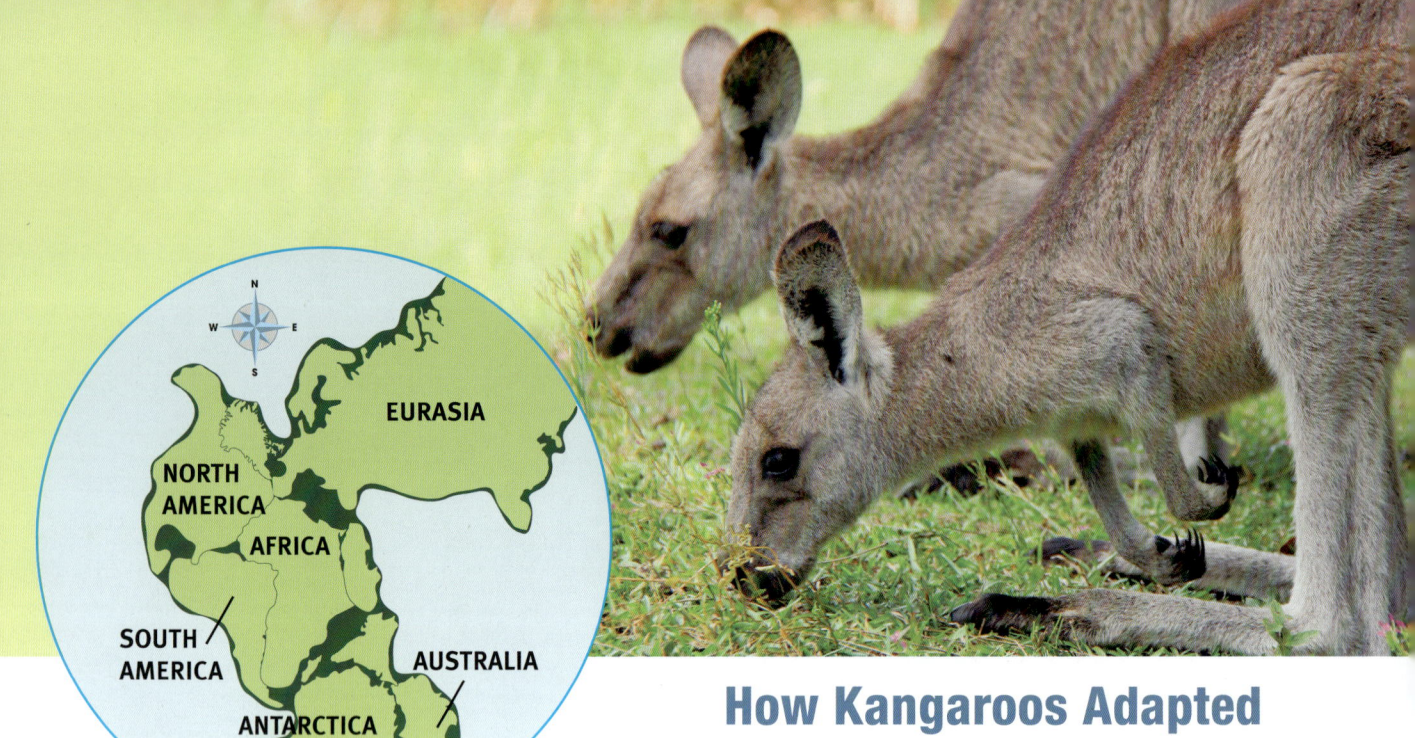

▲ Three hundred million years ago, the world's land masses were joined together in a supercontinent called Pangaea.

At first, Australia was part of Pangaea. Then, about 50 million years ago, it broke away. After that, Australia began to drift very slowly. Today, Australia still moves about 70 millimeters (almost 3 inches) northeast each year.

At about the same time, the ancestors of the kangaroo moved from South America through Antarctica to Australia.

How Kangaroos Adapted to Their New Home

About 15 million years ago, Australia went from warm and wet to cold and dry. As a result, kangaroos had to adapt. First, they changed their diet. They went from eating woody vegetation in wet climates to grazing on grasses in dry climates. As kangaroos evolved, they grew teeth.

Kangaroos also had to adapt to drought conditions. They learned to get through long periods with very little water. Kangaroos today can still go for months without water. Some species don't need water at all if fresh green grass is available.

Hop to It, 'Roo

Thousands of years ago, the ancestors of kangaroos didn't hop. They walked upright on two feet, says Christine Janis. She is a professor of ecology at Brown University. She studies living things and their environment. She believes that kangaroos learned to hop to get away from predators.

When a kangaroo's large feet hit the ground, it's like a spring pressing down. Then the feet snap back up, pushing the kangaroo forward. Some kangaroos can hop 48 kph (30 mph). They can cover 8 meters (25 feet) in a single leap.

◀ A prehistoric kangaroo was as much as 2 m (7 ft.) tall and could weigh 240 kg (529 lb.). A red kangaroo today is about 1.5 m (5 ft.) and can weigh 90 kg (almost 200 lb.).

The Vanishing Marsupials of Australia

Kangaroos and wallabies are plentiful in Australia. Other Australian marsupials, however, are endangered. Here are some ways they are being helped.

The northern hairy-nosed wombat grows to 1 m (3 ft. 3 in.) long and weighs up to 40 kg (88 lb.).

The Tasmanian devil has a very strong bite and a very loud screeching bark.

Northern Hairy-Nosed Wombat

In 1982, only thirty-two northern hairy-nosed wombats lived in the wild. Scientists were afraid they would die off. They fenced in the wombat's habitat. That kept predators out. By 2012, the number of wombats had grown to 200.

Tasmanian Devil

The world's largest meat-eating marsupial is found only on the Australian island state of Tasmania. The animal's population dropped from around 150,000 in 1995 to around 50,000 in 2006 due to a rare disease. Scientists are working on a cure.

Clermont, Queensland
AUSTRALIA
N W E S
The colored areas are the current habitats of these endangered animals.
Tasmania

northern hairy-nosed wombat
koala
Tasmanian devil

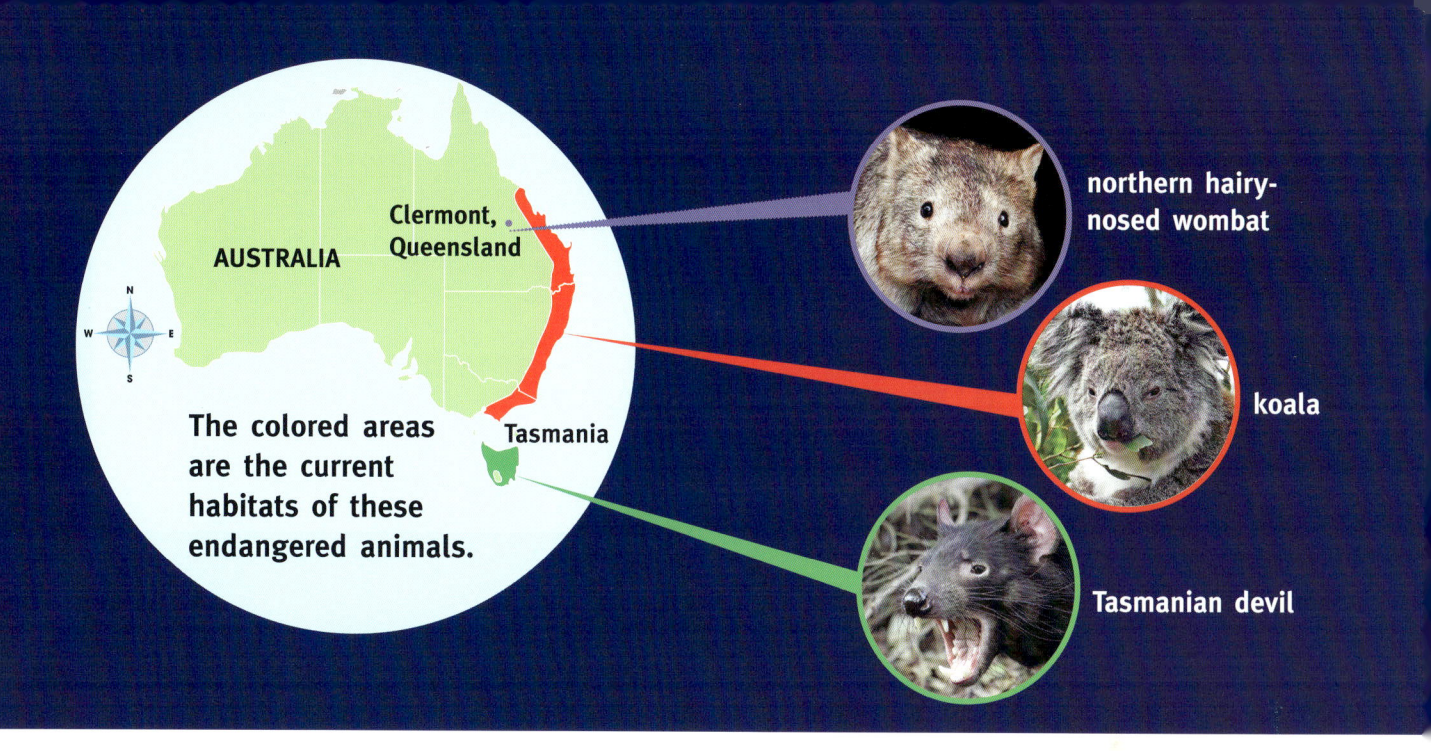

Koala

The Australian Koala Foundation estimates that 43,000 koalas live in Australia. That number is shrinking, though, because koalas eat only eucalyptus leaves. Over the years, people have cut down these trees to start farms or build towns. Koalas are now being helped in a number of ways.

1. The Australian government passed laws to protect koalas' habitats.

2. Eucalyptus trees have been planted in areas where koalas live.

3. Schools raise money to give to the Australian Koala Foundation.

▲ Koalas eat only eucalyptus leaves. They face loss of habitat and food supply.

Animal Survival Today
When an Ecosystem Changes

An ecosystem is the natural environment where plants and animals live. It can be as small as a mud puddle. Or it can be a very large place, such as a rain forest.

The plants and animals that make up an ecosystem depend on one another for survival. They also depend on nonliving features of the environment. These include water, sun, and the weather. According to the Environmental Protection Agency (EPA), "Losing one species in an ecosystem can affect many others."

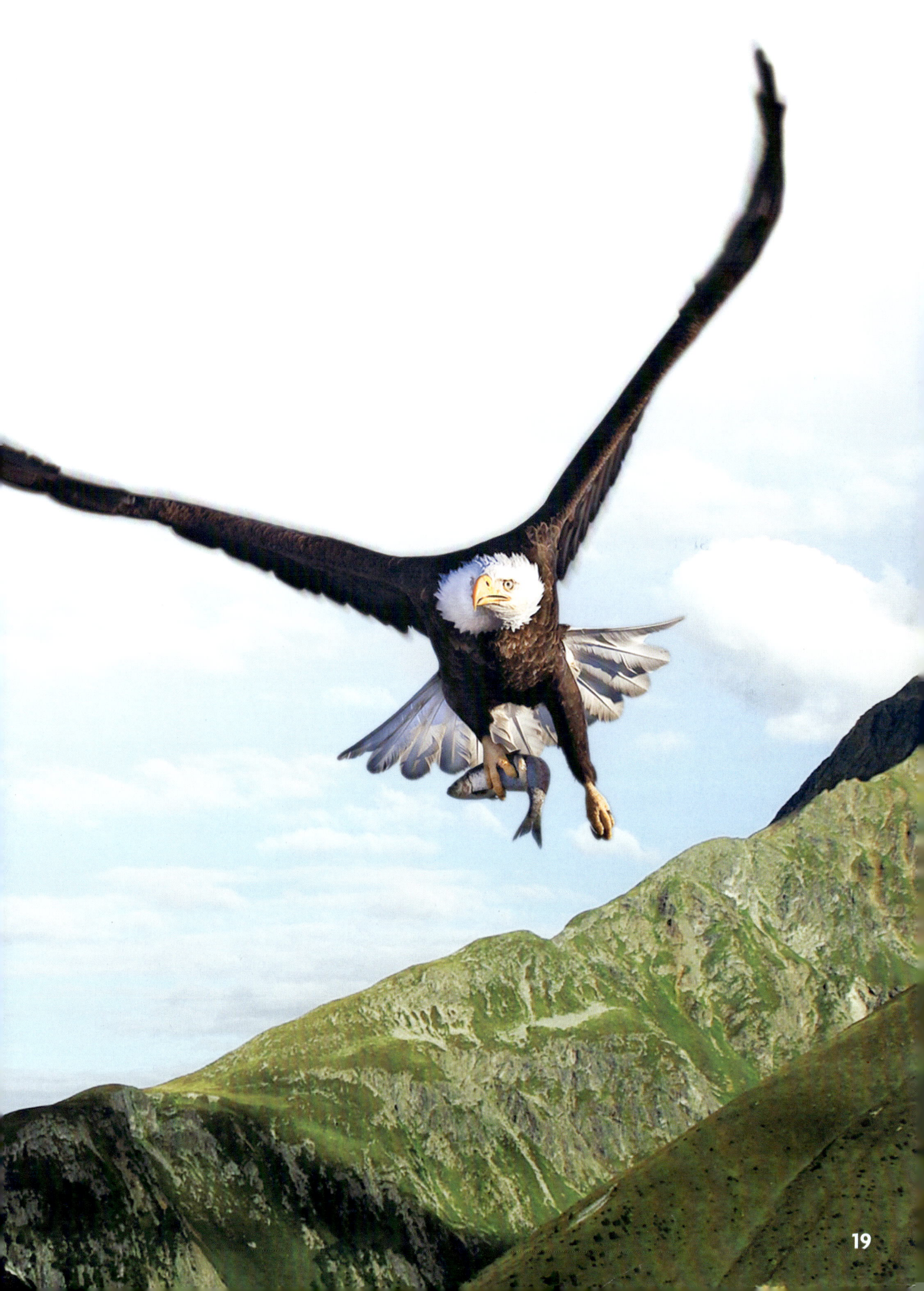

Wolves, Elk, and Songbirds in Yellowstone Park

In the early 1900s, many wolves lived in Yellowstone National Park. The wolves were predators of elk. They kept the elk population from growing too large. By 1926, human hunters had killed the last wolf pack in Yellowstone. As a result, the elk population increased. That caused problems.

Elk eat willow trees. With many more elk in Yellowstone, the willows started to disappear. So did the songbirds that made their homes in the willows. The ecosystem was out of balance.

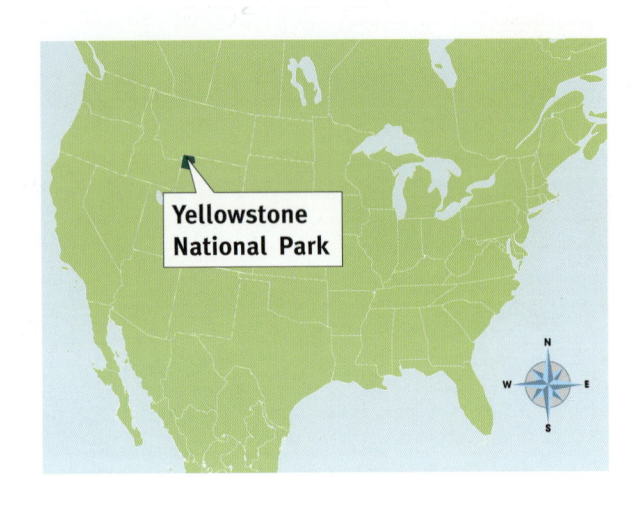

In 1995, scientists reintroduced wolves to Yellowstone. The wolves reduced the elk population. Today, willow trees are plentiful and songbirds have returned.

What Causes an Ecosystem to Change?

Ecosystems are made of living and nonliving things. They change for two general reasons. One is a natural event, such as a fire or flood. A flood, for example, can force many wild animals to flee their natural habitat.

Human activity can also change an ecosystem. Deforestation—the cutting down of trees—is one such example. According to the World Wildlife Fund (WWF), eight of ten species on Earth live in forests. When forests are cut down, these species lose their homes. They either adapt or die off.

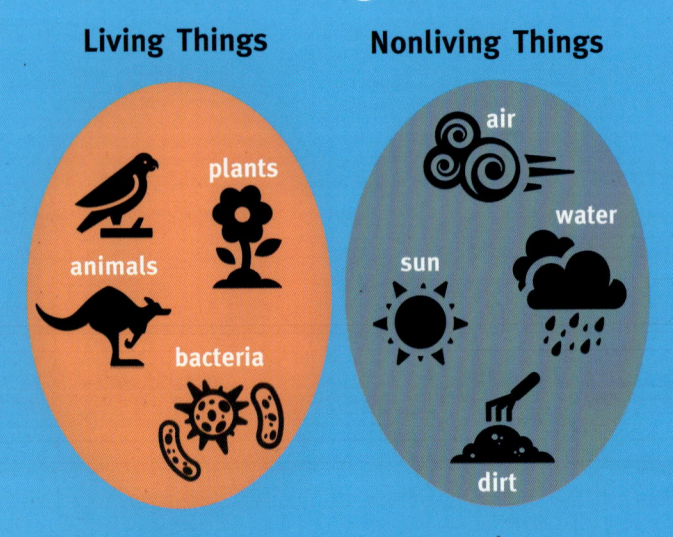

Living Things: animals, plants, bacteria

Nonliving Things: air, water, sun, dirt

Endangered!

Change in an ecosystem, whether from natural events or human activity, can affect the animals that live there in two main ways. First, it destroys the animals' habitat. Second, it often causes animals to lose their food supply. Either can result in an animal being put on an endangered species list. Here are two:

Lemur

The lemur is a small monkey. Lemurs live only in Madagascar, an island country near Africa. A grown male weighs about 2.5 kg (5.5 lb.). Millions of years ago, lemurs were as large as adult gorillas. They lived on the ground.

Lemurs now mostly live in trees. Scientists believe lemurs grew smaller over time to adapt to living in trees. Yet much of the lemur's tree habitat is being destroyed. Ten years ago, 10 of the 113 lemur species were critically endangered. Today, over 90 percent of lemur species are at a risk for extinction.

The lemur is in the monkey family, but it looks like a cross between a cat and a squirrel.

The Iberian lynx is around 1 meter long (about 3 feet). A grown male weighs around 13 kg (28 lb.).

Iberian Lynx

The Iberian lynx is a medium-sized wildcat. In the early 1800s, thousands lived in the forests of Spain and Portugal. Today, scientists believe only a few hundred remain. The WWF reports that it is the most endangered mammal in Europe.

A main reason the Iberian lynx is dying off is loss of food supply. It rarely eats anything other than rabbit. Yet the rabbits in the Iberian lynx's ecosystem are being hunted by humans. The rabbits are also dying from a disease. As a result, the lynx population continues to drop. To add to their problems, high-speed roads now pass through their habitat. In 2014, twenty-two lynxes were killed by cars.

Protect Endangered Animals

The loss of even one animal species can lead to changes in an ecosystem and cause problems for other animals. Some countries have made it illegal to capture, kill, or harm endangered animals. Others are working to protect the ecosystems of those animals. Many zoos around the world now have special programs to breed endangered animals.

Here are three success stories from the United States:

👍 The Endangered Species Act protects more than 2,000 plants and animals. Many endangered animals are now doing much better because of its laws. The whooping crane, for instance, was down to only two dozen in the 1940s. More than 400 live in the wild today.

👍 The National Zoo in Washington, D.C., started a mating program for black-footed ferrets in 1991. Once thought extinct, more than 600 black-footed ferrets have been born at the zoo.

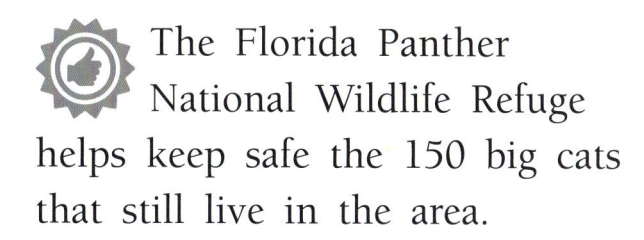

👍 The Florida Panther National Wildlife Refuge helps keep safe the 150 big cats that still live in the area.

SAVE THE ANIMAL PROGRAMS

TYPE	EXAMPLE (YEAR STARTED)	
National Law	Endangered Species Act (1973)	whooping crane
Recovery Program	National Zoo's Conservation Biology Institute (1991)	black-footed ferret
National Park	Florida Panther National Wildlife Refuge (1989)	panther

Glossary

ancestors (AN-ses-terz) *noun* relatives who lived in the past

breed (BREED) *verb* to produce by mixing together

ecosystem (EE-koh-sis-tem) *noun* a community of living things that work together to make up an environment

endangered (in-DANE-jerd) *adjective* almost extinct

evolved (ih-VAHLVD) *verb* experienced developmental changes over time

extinct (ik-STINGKT) *adjective* no longer existing, such as an animal species

fossil (FAH-sul) *noun* the remains or traces of a living organism from an earlier time

mammals (MA-mulz) *noun* animals that feed milk to their young

marsupial (mar-SOO-pee-ul) *noun* an animal, such as the kangaroo, that carries its babies in a pouch on the mother's stomach

predators (PREH-duh-terz) *noun* animals that live by killing and eating other animals

prey (PRAY) *noun* an animal that is hunted or killed by another for food

species (SPEE-sheez) *noun* a class of living things that are related and share similar characteristics and qualities

Index

Australia, 12–14, 16–17

Canada, 7

Endangered Species Act, 23

Environmental Protection agency (EPA), 18

Ice Age, 4–11

Madagascar, 21

megafauna, 6–7

North America, 6, 8–9

Pangaea, 13–14

Portugal, 22

Spain, 22

Tasmania, 16

World Wildlife Fund (WWF), 20, 22

Yellowstone National Park, 20